Easy-to-Make
ARTICULATED WOODEN TOYS

Patterns and Instructions for 18 Playthings That Move

ED SIBBETT, JR.

Dover Publications, Inc., New York

INSTRUCTIONS

The articulated wooden toys presented in this book combine action, color and fun in a wonderful variety of shapes and subjects. Dragons, wild horses, honey bears, clowns, parrots and circus girls join arms, clap hands, tap heels and kick up their feet in a carnival of moving parts. They climb, dance, do somersaults, jumping jacks and handstands, rock, roll, swing and walk. Assembled correctly, these sturdy toys will retain their charm for a lifetime and more, looking as fresh and lively as the day they were made.

Inside this book are patterns and instructions for making the eighteen toys pictured on the covers. All of these easy-to-assemble projects can be made with the materials listed below. The toy patterns are printed on inked transfer paper and can be ironed onto wood, eliminating much of the need for tracing. Once the pattern pieces are transferred onto wood of the appropriate thickness, they can be cut out along the outside line. The design to be painted on the pieces is illustrated by the solid interior lines. Dots indicate the width and position of holes to be drilled in the wood surface. Dotted lines mark positions for gluing or nailing. Dashed lines indicate holes to be drilled in the center of side surfaces.

The toys are presented in general order of complexity. The pattern key boxed off within the instructions for each toy lists the parts needed in the construction of the model. Refer to the key for the correct thickness of the wood onto which to transfer each piece of the pattern. Pattern pieces are identified by the letters in the box and the corresponding ones on the transfer sheets. Dowels, wire, string and rope are used to construct the joints,

axles, rollers and pullstrings that animate the toys. Plates 9, 13 and 14 include diagrams showing details of the moving features.

You may paint the toys using the paint lines as guides or choose your own design. Some pieces in the patterns will need designs either traced or sketched freehand on their back after they are cut out. For toys like the Rocking Horse (Plate 3) that require the same design on both sides, paint lines can be traced onto the back surface. The Climbing Circus Girl (Plate 1) and Dancing Man (Plate 14) will need to have a design sketched on their back surface that complements the front.

MATERIALS

Pine shelving or plywood, ³⁄₃₂″, ⅛″, ¼″, ½″ and ¾″ in thickness (finished widths)

Table-mounted scroll saw or jigsaw (hand-held power saws will not give satisfactory results, but skilled craftsmen may be able to cut some of the projects with a coping saw)

Drill and ¹⁄₃₂″ to ⁵⁄₁₆″ bits

Iron

Medium and fine sandpaper

Paints (acrylics, poster paints, etc.) or marking pens

Dowels, ⅛″, ³⁄₁₆″ and ¼″ in diameter

Heavy wire, string or rope

Glue

Carbon paper, tracing paper and pen, pencil or stylus

■ ■ ■ ■

Published in Canada by General Publishing Company, Ltd., 30 Lesmill Road, Don Mills, Toronto, Ontario.
Published in the United Kingdom by Constable and Company, Ltd.

Easy-to-Make Articulated Wooden Toys: Patterns and Instructions for 18 Playthings That Move is a new work, first published by Dover Publications, Inc., in 1983.

Manufactured in the United States of America
Dover Publications, Inc., 31 East 2nd Street, Mineola, N.Y. 11501

Library of Congress Cataloging in Publication Data

Sibbett, Ed.
   Easy-to-make articulated wooden toys.

   1. Wooden toy making.   I. Title.
TT174.5.W6S5   1983   745.592   82-9537
ISBN 0-486-24411-3 (pbk.)

GENERAL INSTRUCTIONS

Beginning craftsmen should refer to woodworking manuals to learn proper cutting and drilling techniques.

1. Select pieces of raw, unfinished wood that are free from knots and blemishes for all thicknesses required in the pattern. Hobby and craft stores sell wood in finished widths. Wood bought at hardware and lumber stores is usually sold by prefinished widths, which may be ⅛" to ¼" narrower than wood in finished widths. Specify to the salesperson that the measurements you are requesting are finished sizes. Gently sand all surfaces onto which you will be transferring patterns with medium and fine sandpaper until wood is smooth. Dust with a tack cloth.

2. Following the directions given below, iron each piece of the transfer pattern onto wood of the specified thickness. Some pieces will need to be transferred more than once.

3. Cut out all pieces, following the outside lines on the patterns.

4. Following the directions given below, trace or sketch the design on the back surface of the cut-out pieces. This step is not necessary for pieces containing few paint lines.

5. Cut out dowels and drill holes of specified lengths and widths.

6. Sand the rough edges very gently. You may smooth all surfaces with fine sandpaper, but be careful to retain paint lines and other transfer marks.

7. Paint the pieces using the paint lines as guides. Larger areas should be painted first; smaller areas can be painted over the large areas when the paint dries. Tiny areas such as eyes and mouths can be added with a marking pen. If you prefer using markers for the entire toy, be sure to use a permanent marker. Test the markers by applying the colors to a piece of scrap wood and then holding the wood under water after the marker has dried. If the color runs, the marker is not permanent. Any areas you leave unpainted should be sanded free of transfer ink.

8. Assemble the toy as instructed using dowels, glue, wire, string or rope.

TRANSFERRING THE PATTERNS

Before beginning any project it is a good idea to test your iron, the wood and the evenness of your hand pressure. Cut out one of the test squares on Plates 1, 7 or 11 and follow the directions below for transferring. Since these transfer patterns are permanent, make certain that your test square is transferred onto a piece of scrap wood. If the ink transfers well, you can proceed; if not, adjust either the heat or length of pressing time.

1. Use a dry iron set at the hottest temperature.

2. Place the piece of wood on a solid surface.

3. Remove the page or cut out the pattern pieces, leaving a margin around the edges of each pattern for taping and tacking. For some toys all the pattern pieces can be transferred onto one board; on others the pieces will have to be separated according to the thickness of wood onto which they will be transferred. Refer to each toy's pattern key to arrange the pieces on wood of correct thickness. Tape or tack patterns to wood, inked side down, making sure that patterns are secure to prevent movement and subsequent blurring of design. However, if you are using tape, free space must be left along one edge of the design for iron to be used. A hot iron will be ruined by melted tape, so exercise extreme caution when placing iron near the edges of design. Protect the iron with a sheet of tissue paper between transfer and iron.

4. Place the heated iron on a transfer pattern and press down for about 5 seconds. Apply firm, even pressure to all parts of the design, being especially careful to get the outer edges (without pressing over tape). Do not move iron back and forth across the wood as this will cause the transfer to blur. The time required for transferring the design will increase 2–3 seconds each time the transfer is reused. You can usually get four or more transfers from each pattern.

5. Carefully remove one fastener and lift the transfer paper to see whether the complete design is indicated on the wood. If not, replace the fastener and repeat the process. Do not remove all the fasteners until the entire design has been successfully transferred. Once the pattern has been removed it is almost impossible to register it on the wood again. Repeat the transferring process for each pattern piece. Some of the patterns will need to be taped down and transferred more than once.

6. Remove the tacks or tape when you are satisfied that the transferring is completed. Save the transfer paper for reference purposes and for making additional transfers if you wish another copy of the toy. If the design is not clear enough, you can reinforce areas with a pencil.

TRACING THE DESIGN

If you do not want to use an iron for transferring the designs, or if you wish to trace the paint lines on the back of a piece, the patterns can be transferred with tracing and carbon paper. Put a piece of tracing paper over the uninked side of the transfer and trace the patterns and identification letters. If the patterns are to be cut out of different thicknesses of wood, use a separate sheet of tracing paper for the pieces of each thickness. Tack the traced designs to the wood and slip a piece of carbon paper, color-side down, between the wood and the tracing; do not tack carbon. With a hard, even pressure, trace a few lines with a pencil, stylus or similar tool. Raise one corner of the tracing and the carbon to check the impression. If the results are too faint, apply more pressure; if too heavy, apply less pressure. Trace all the lines and then remove the carbon and carefully remove one tack to see whether the patterns are intact on the wood before removing the tracing. Be especially careful to differentiate between the solid, dashed and dotted lines.

To transfer the paint lines to the back of a cut-out piece, flop a tracing of the pattern (so that letters are inverted) and carefully adjust design until it fits wood piece correctly. Insert tacks very lightly through tracing into wood piece at the tips so that there is sufficient room for a suitably cut piece of carbon paper to be slipped under the tracing. If tack holes are objectionable to you, rolled-up masking tape stuck to the wood piece's side surfaces can be used to attach tracing to wood piece. Next, gently but with firm pressure transfer the design onto the wood, adjusting the carbon if necessary as you trace the lines. Check impression at edges before completely removing tracing material.

■ ■ ■ ■

DO NOT GIVE PAINTED TOYS TO YOUNG CHILDREN WHO HAVE A TENDENCY TO PUT THINGS IN THEIR MOUTHS.

CLIMBING CIRCUS GIRL

(The transfer patterns for this toy are printed on Plate 1.)

Pull on one cord and then the other. With each pull the circus girl climbs a little higher. When she arrives at the top, let go of the cords and she will slide down to the bottom, ready for another climb.

4 pattern pieces, 2 pieces of heavy wire, 3 pieces of string.

PATTERN KEY

A. balance bar, ½"   B. body, ¼"   C. left leg, ¼"
D. right leg, ¼"

Dashed lines indicate ³⁄₃₂" holes to be drilled in side surface of hands.
Dots indicate ³⁄₃₂" holes to be drilled in balance bar, body and legs.

1. Transfer all patterns onto wood of specified thickness.
2. Cut out all wood pattern pieces.
3. Sketch an appropriate pattern on back of body and feet.
4. Drill holes where indicated by dashed lines and dots.
5. Sand rough edges on wood pieces.
6. Paint all wood pattern pieces.
7. Attach legs to body. Cut 1" piece of wire and bend one end over to form a knot. Insert other end through holes in right leg and body and bend it into a knot. Repeat procedure for left leg.
8. To form a holder for the toy, insert a 3" length of string in center hole of balance bar and tie knots in both ends of string.
9. Tie a knot in the end of an 18" length of string. Insert other end through a hole in the balance bar and one of the hands and tie a knot in end of string. Repeat procedure for other hand.

WILD HORSE

(The transfer patterns for this toy are printed on Plate 2.)

5 pattern pieces, 2 pieces of heavy wire, 3 pieces of string.

PATTERN KEY

A. horse, ¾″   B, C, D, E. wheels, ½″

Two ³⁄₁₆″ dowels of 1¾″ length for wheels.

Dots indicate ³⁄₁₆″ holes to be drilled in wheels and ¼″ holes in horse.

1. Transfer the patterns onto wood of specified thickness.
2. Cut out all wood pattern pieces.
3. Trace paint lines onto opposite side of horse.
4. Cut dowels.
5. Drill holes where indicated by dots.
6. Sand rough edges on wood pieces.
7. Paint all wood pattern pieces.
8. Attach wheels to horse by inserting dowels.

■ ■ ■ ■

ROCKING HORSE
WITH HONEY BEAR

(The transfer patterns for this toy are printed on Plate 3.)

8 pattern pieces, 6 dowels.

PATTERN KEY

A. honey bear, ¾″   B. rocking horse, ¾″   C, D. rockers, ½″
E, F. arms, ¼″   G, H. legs, ¼″

Two ³⁄₁₆″ dowels of 1¼″ length for arms and legs of bear; two ³⁄₁₆″ dowels of 1½″ length for crossbars in neck and body of horse; two ³⁄₁₆″ dowels of 1¾″ length for rockers.

Dots indicate ³⁄₁₆″ holes to be drilled in bear, horse and rockers and ¼″ holes in horse's feet.

1. Transfer the patterns onto wood of specified thickness.
2. Cut out all wood pattern pieces.
3. Trace paint lines onto opposite side of horse.
4. Cut dowels.
5. Drill holes where indicated by dots.
6. Sand rough edges on wood pieces.
7. Paint all wood pattern pieces.
8. Assemble rocking horse and honey bear by inserting dowels in appropriate holes.

CIRCUS WAGON

(The transfer patterns for this toy are printed on Plate 4.)

11 pattern pieces, 22 dowels.

PATTERN KEY

All pieces on ½" wood.

A. wagon base

B, C. wheel supports

D, E. wagon tops (long sides)

F, G. wagon tops (short sides)

H, I, J, K. wheels

Two ³⁄₁₆" dowels of 5½" length for wheels; twenty ¼" dowels of 4½" length to connect base and tops of wagon.

Dashed lines indicate ¼" holes to be drilled in side surface of wheel supports and wagon tops.

Dots indicate ¼" holes to be drilled in wagon base and wagon tops, and ³⁄₁₆" holes in wheels.

1. Transfer all patterns onto wood of specified thickness.
2. Cut out all wood pattern pieces.
3. Cut dowels.
4. Drill holes where indicated by dots and dashed lines.
5. Sand rough edges on wood pieces.
6. Paint all wood pattern pieces.
7. Glue wheel supports under long sides of wagon base. The ends of the supports should be ½" from the ends of the wagon base. The holes in the supports on both sides should align so that dowel axles fit properly.
8. Glue the twenty shorter dowels into wagon base.
9. Glue the four wagon top pieces on top of dowels.
10. Attach wheels with remaining two dowels.
11. Attach screw eye to wagon base if you wish to pull the toy by a string.

■ ■ ■ ■

CIRCUS ANIMALS

(The transfer patterns for these toys are printed on Plate 5.)

3 pattern pieces.

PATTERN KEY

All pieces on ¾" wood.

A. giraffe   B. elephant   C. lion

---

1. Transfer all patterns onto wood of specified thickness.
2. Cut out all wood pattern pieces.
3. Sand rough edges on wood pieces.
4. Paint all wood pattern pieces. Paint eyes on animals.

ROLLING CLOWN

(The transfer patterns for this toy are printed on Plate 6.)

5 pattern pieces, 6 dowels.

PATTERN KEY

All pieces on ½" wood.

A. rolling clown   B, C. roll bar rails   D, E. feet of rack

One ¼" dowel of 6½" length to connect feet of rack; four ¼" dowels of 4" length to connect rails to feet; one ¼" dowel of 2½" length for clown's roller.

Dashed lines indicate ¼" holes to be drilled in side surface of rack feet and rollers. Dots indicate ¼" holes to be drilled in clown and feet of rack.

1. Transfer all patterns onto wood of specified thickness.
2. Cut out all wood pattern pieces.
3. Trace paint lines onto opposite side of clown.
4. Cut dowels.
5. Drill holes where indicated by dashed lines and dots.
6. Sand rough edges on wood pieces. The curves in the rails should be smooth and even to make clown roll properly.
7. Paint all wood pattern pieces.
8. Place short dowel through clown's hands.
9. Assemble rolling rack by gluing dowels into rails and feet of rack in appropriate places. Small knobs glued on the ends of rails will keep clown from rolling off.

■ ■ ■ ■

BALANCE BIRD

(The transfer patterns for this toy are printed on Plate 7.)

5 pattern pieces.

PATTERN KEY

All parts on ¼" wood.

A. balance bird   B, C. right weights   D, E. left weights

Dotted line indicates position to glue weights.

1. Transfer all patterns onto wood of specified thickness.
2. Cut out all wood pattern pieces.
3. Trace paint lines onto opposite side of balance bird.
4. Sand rough edges on all pieces.
5. Paint all wood pattern pieces.
6. Glue weights to indicated position on tail of bird, two on right side and two on left.

BALANCING ACROBATS

(The transfer patterns for this toy are printed on Plate 8.)

10 pattern pieces, 5 dowels.

PATTERN KEY

A. top acrobat, ¾"   B. bottom acrobat's   C, D. bottom acrobat's
                          middle section, ¾"   outside sections, ³⁄₃₂"

E. acrobats' platform, ½" F. balancing peg, ½"   G, H, I, J. wheels, ¼"

Two ³⁄₁₆" dowels of 3½" length for platform; two ³⁄₁₆" dowels of 1¼" length—one for
the nose hole in the face of the top acrobat and one for the nose holes in the faces
of bottom acrobat and the hole in the lump on the top acrobat's head; one ³⁄₁₆"
dowel of 1" length for peg and lower holes in bottom acrobat.

Dashed lines indicate ¼" holes to be drilled in side surface of platform.
Dots indicate ³⁄₁₆" holes to be drilled in peg, wheels and acrobats' bodies.
Dotted lines indicate position for gluing peg.

1. Transfer all patterns onto wood of specified thickness.
2. Cut out all wood pattern pieces.
3. Trace paint lines onto opposite side of top acrobat. You may also wish to trace
the few paint lines on the bottom acrobat's middle section.
4. Cut dowels.
5. Drill holes where indicated by dashed lines and dots.
6. Sand rough edges on wood pieces.
7. Paint all wood pattern pieces.
8. Glue one bottom acrobat outside section to each side of middle section. Use a
clamp to hold three pieces together. Make sure that the dowel holes are aligned.
9. Sand edges on bottom acrobat again.
10. Glue balancing peg to acrobats' platform, hole up.
11. Assemble toy by placing dowels in appropriate holes (the hole in the lump on
the top acrobat's head should be aligned between nose holes on the two faces of
bottom acrobat).

(Instructions continue after patterns)

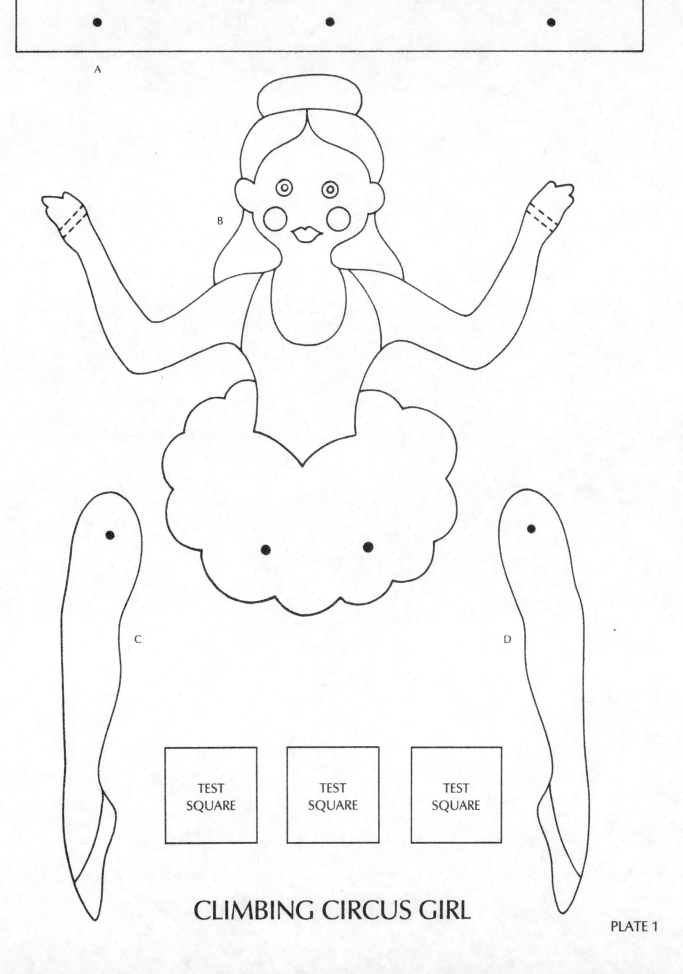

A

B

C

D

TEST
SQUARE

TEST
SQUARE

TEST
SQUARE

CLIMBING CIRCUS GIRL

PLATE 1

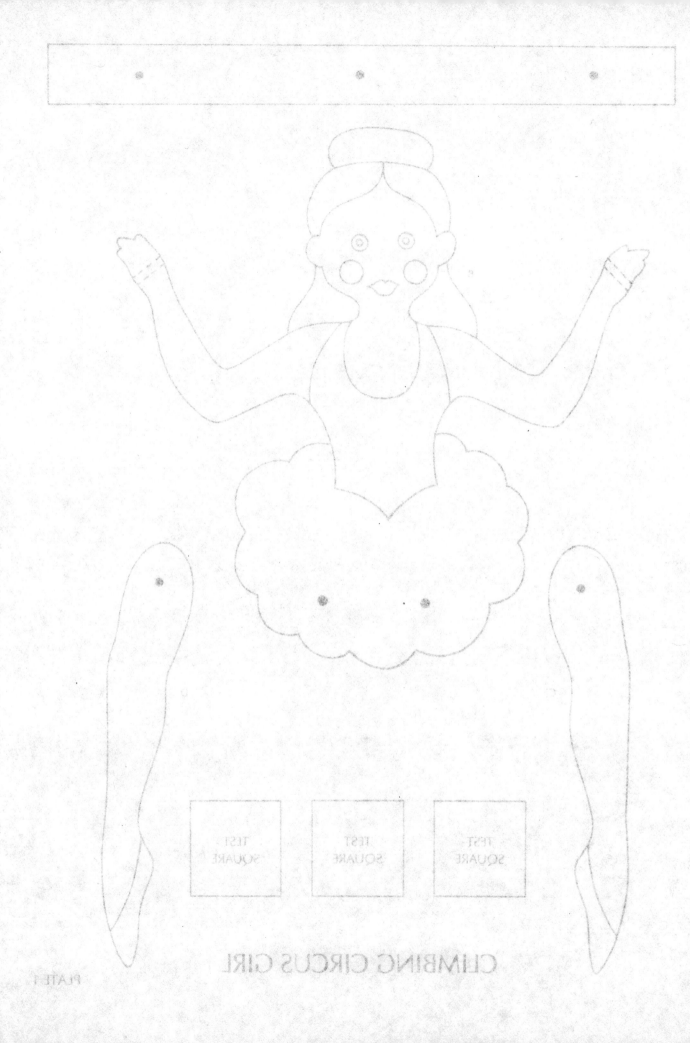

CLIMBING CIRCUS GIRL

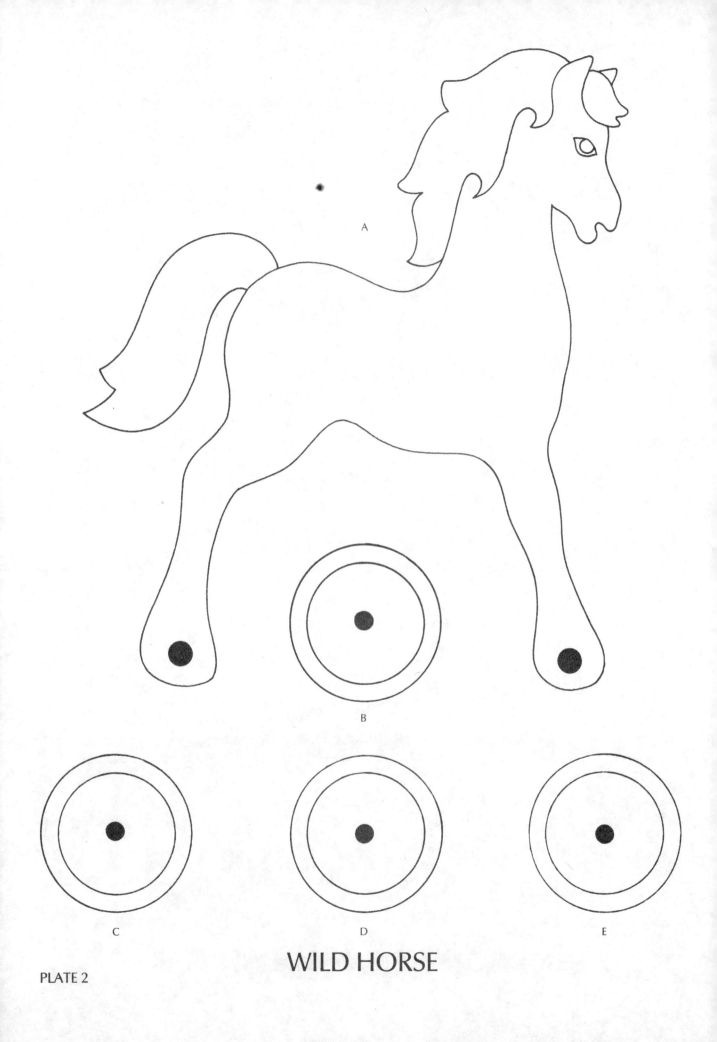

A

B

C   D   E

WILD HORSE

PLATE 2

ROCKING HORSE WITH HONEY BEAR

PLATE 3

ROCKING HORSE WITH HONEY BEAR

PLATE 3

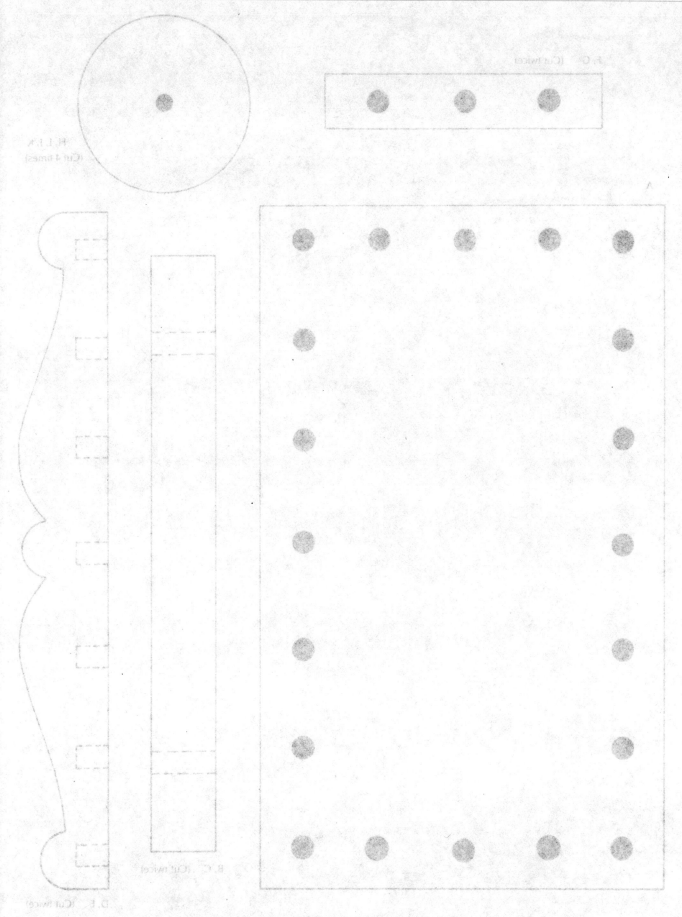

CIRCUS WAGON

PLATE 8

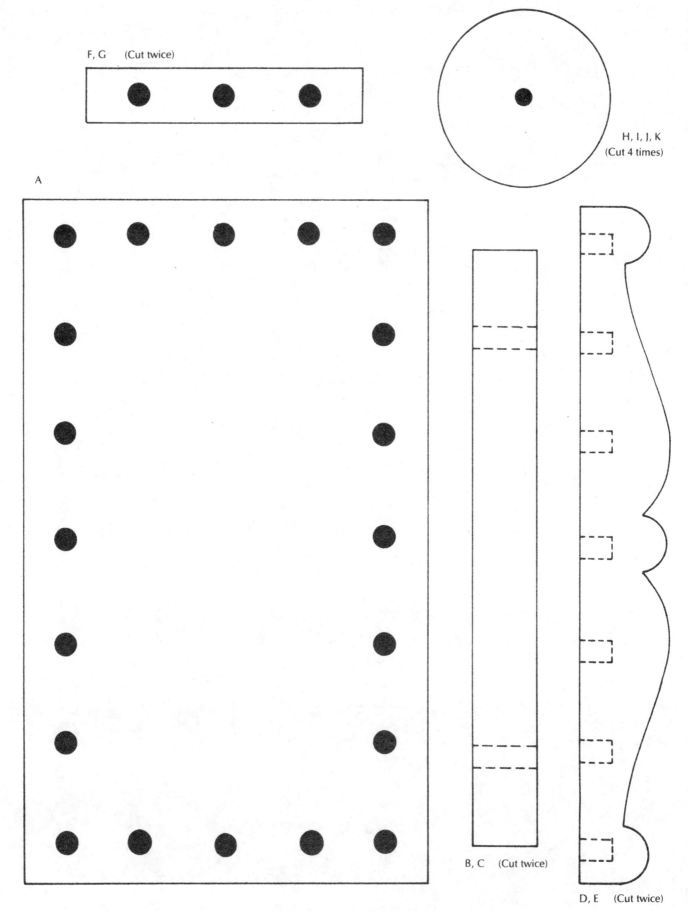

F, G   (Cut twice)

H, I, J, K
(Cut 4 times)

A

B, C   (Cut twice)

D, E   (Cut twice)

CIRCUS WAGON

PLATE 4

CIRCUS ANIMALS

PLATE 5

PLATE 5

ROLLING CLOWN

PLATE 6

B

C

A

D

E

ROLLING CLOWN

PLATE 6

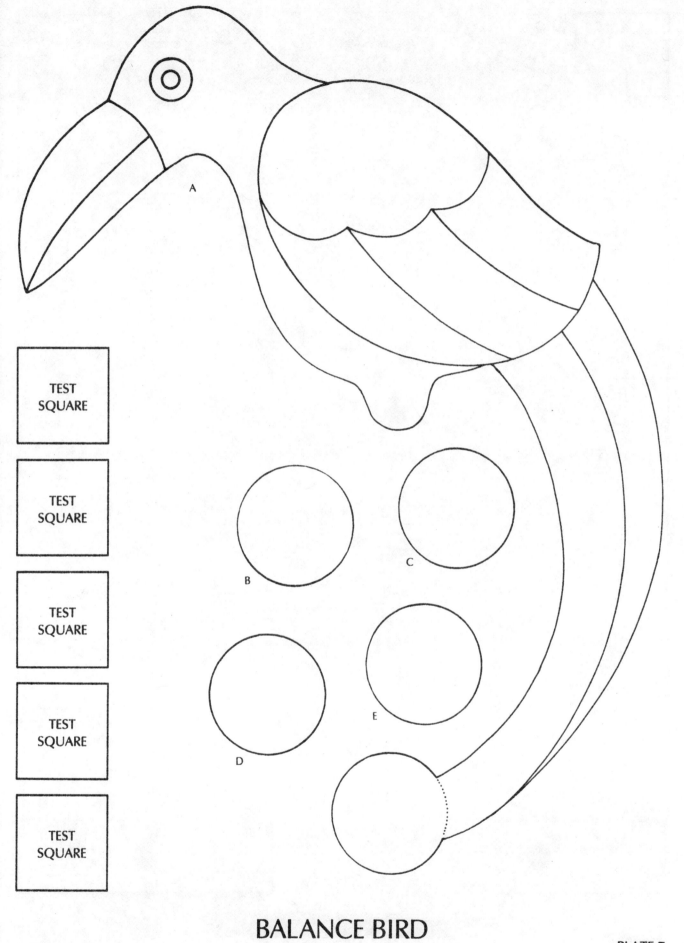

TEST
SQUARE

TEST
SQUARE

TEST
SQUARE

TEST
SQUARE

TEST
SQUARE

A

B

C

D

E

BALANCE BIRD

PLATE 7

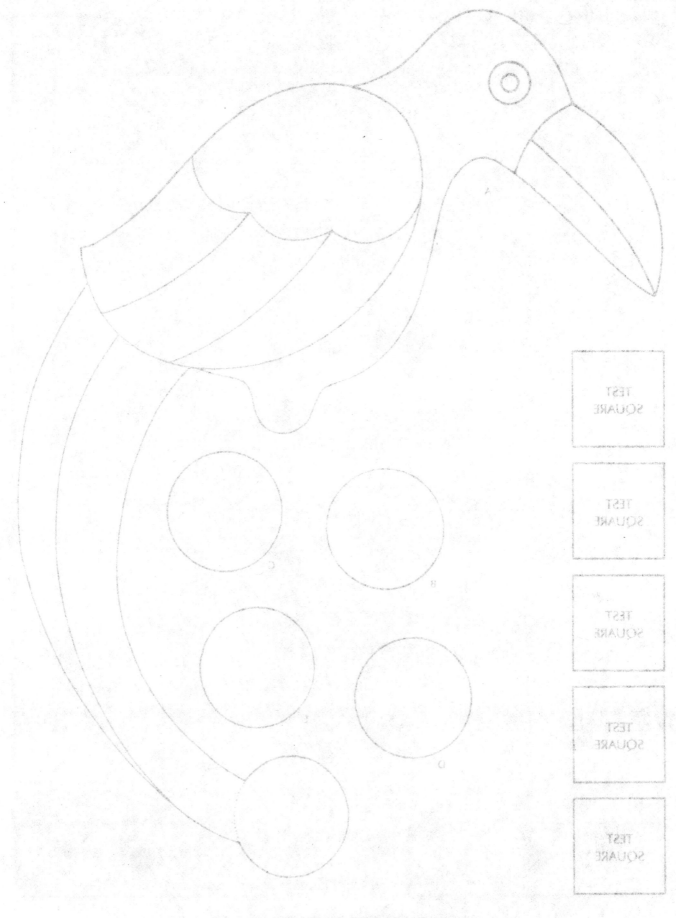

TEST
SQUARE

TEST
SQUARE

TEST
SQUARE

TEST
SQUARE

TEST
SQUARE

BALANCE BIRD

PLATE 7

PLATE 8

A

C, D   (Cut twice)

F

E

B

H

G   J   I

BALANCING ACROBATS

PLATE 8

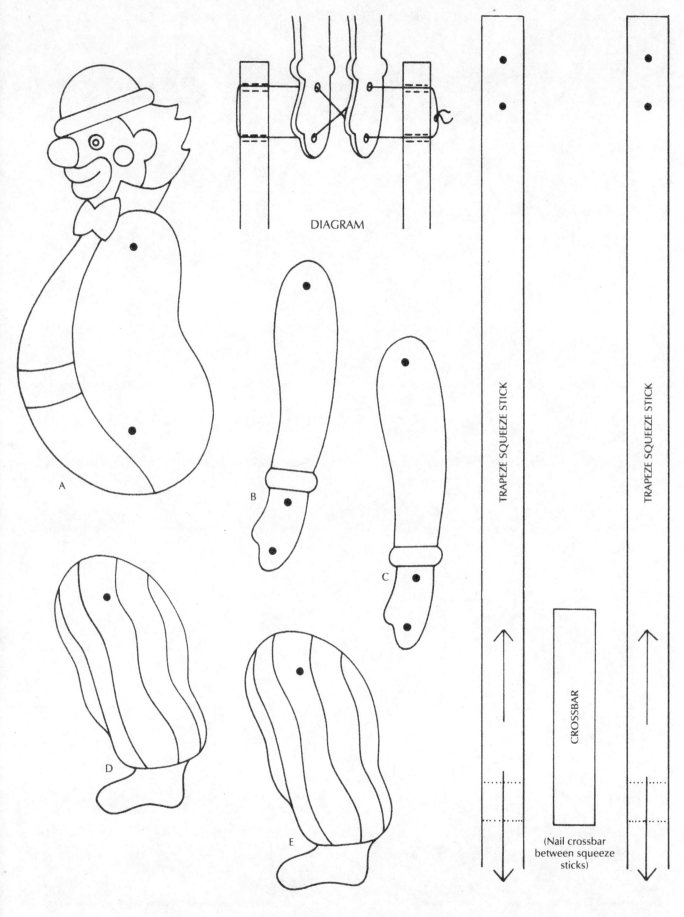

DIAGRAM

A

B

C

D

E

TRAPEZE SQUEEZE STICK

TRAPEZE SQUEEZE STICK

CROSSBAR

(Nail crossbar between squeeze sticks)

ACROBAT CLOWN

PLATE 9

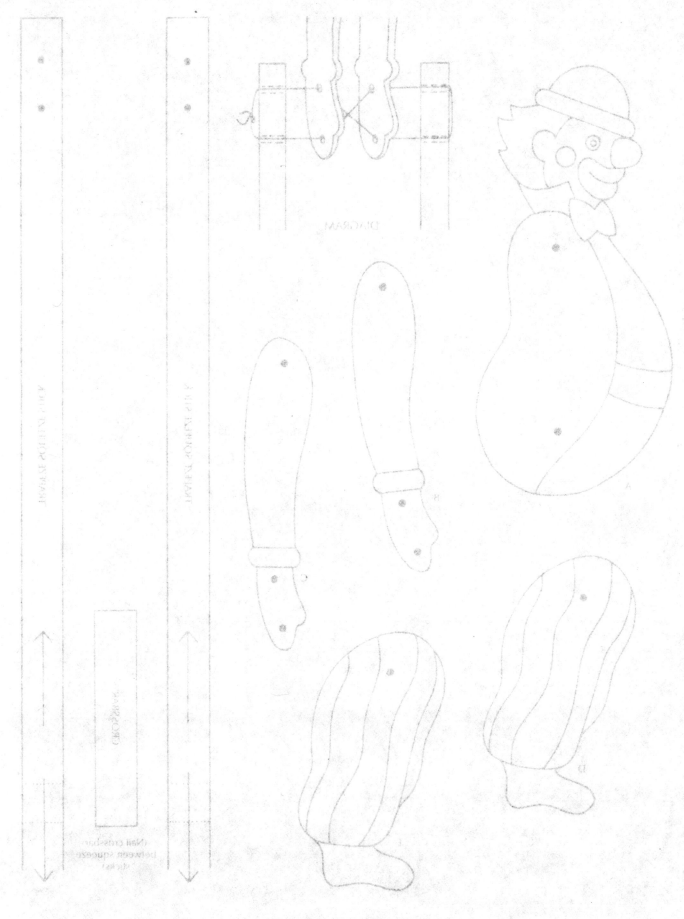

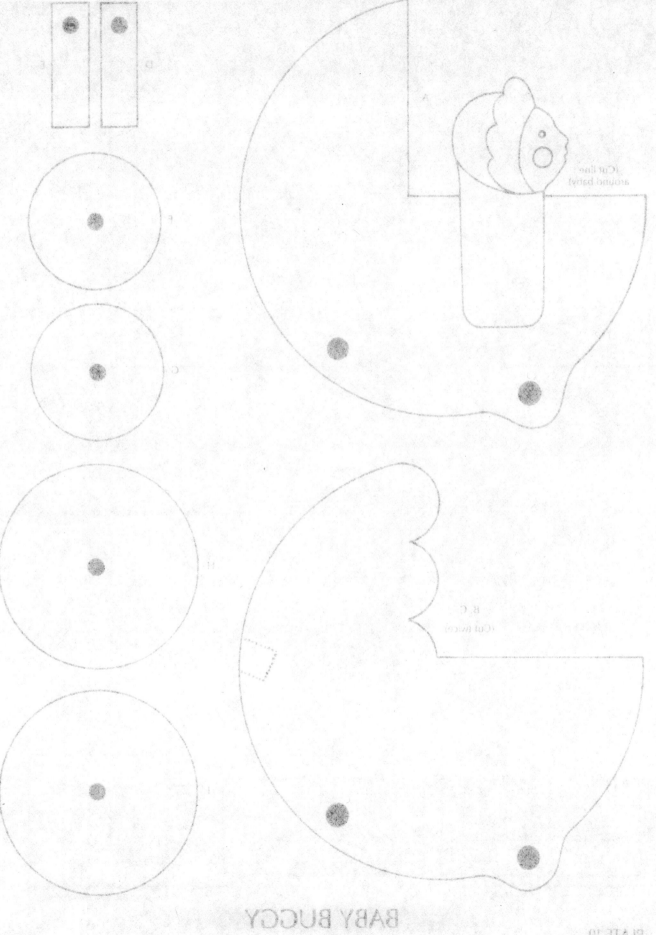

BABY BUGGY

PLATE 10

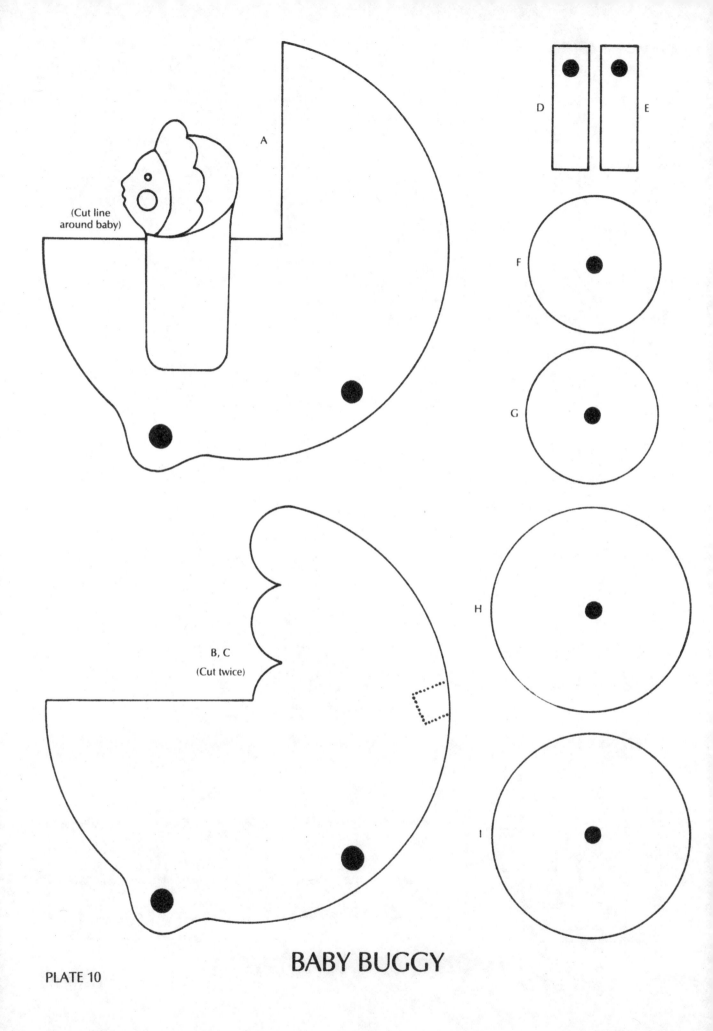

(Cut line around baby)

A

B, C

(Cut twice)

D

E

F

G

H

I

BABY BUGGY

PLATE 10

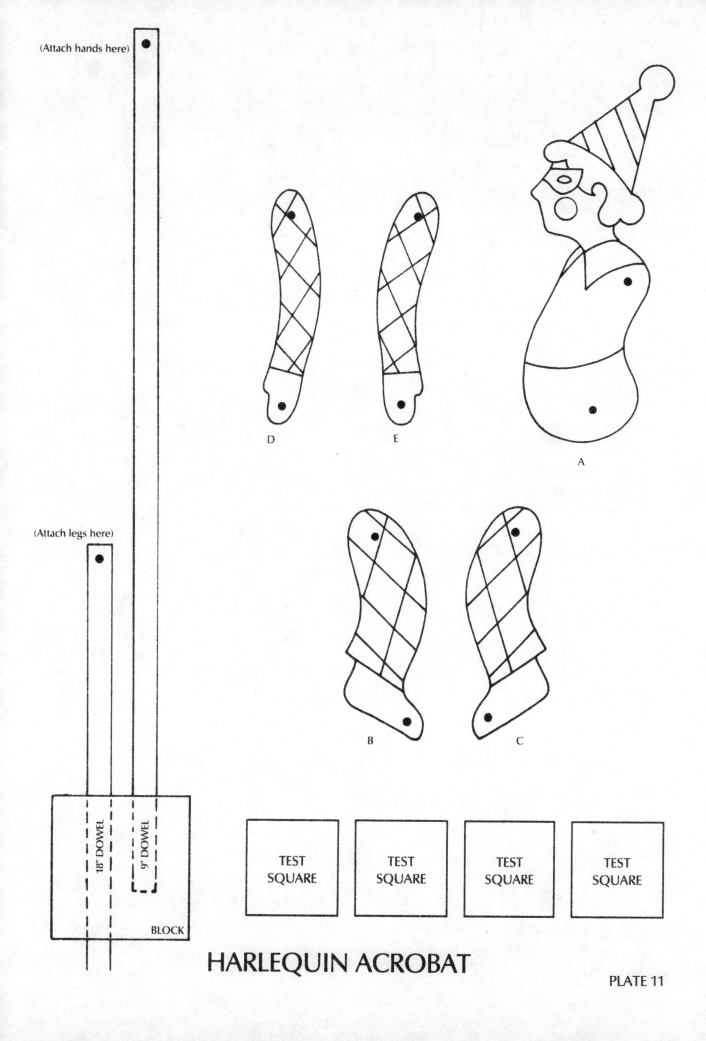

(Attach hands here)

(Attach legs here)

18" DOWEL   9" DOWEL

BLOCK

D   E   A

B   C

TEST SQUARE   TEST SQUARE   TEST SQUARE   TEST SQUARE

HARLEQUIN ACROBAT

PLATE 11

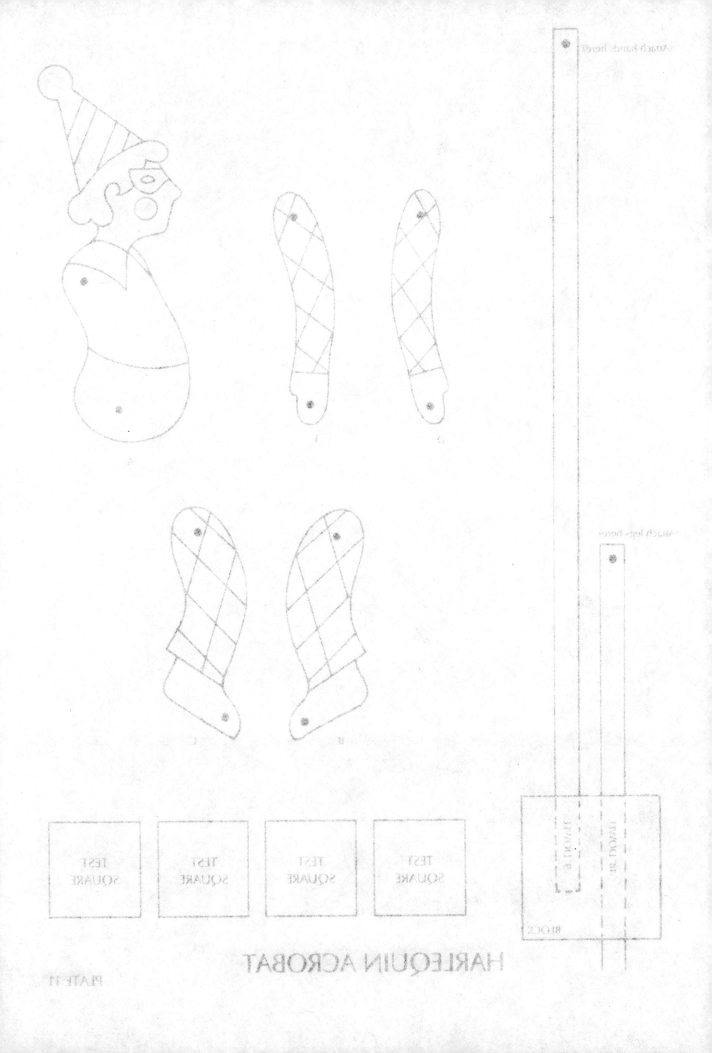

PLATE 11

HARLEQUIN ACROBAT

PARROT SWING BAR

SWINGING PARROT

PLATE 12.

PARROT SWING BAR

LEFT

RIGHT

A

B

LEFT

RIGHT

C

D

x

y

LEFT

RIGHT

SWINGING PARROT

PLATE 12

DIAGRAM

DOWEL NOSE

A

B

C

D

E

F

PINOCCHIO JUMPING JACK

PLATE 13

PINOCCHIO JUMPING JACK

PLATE 13

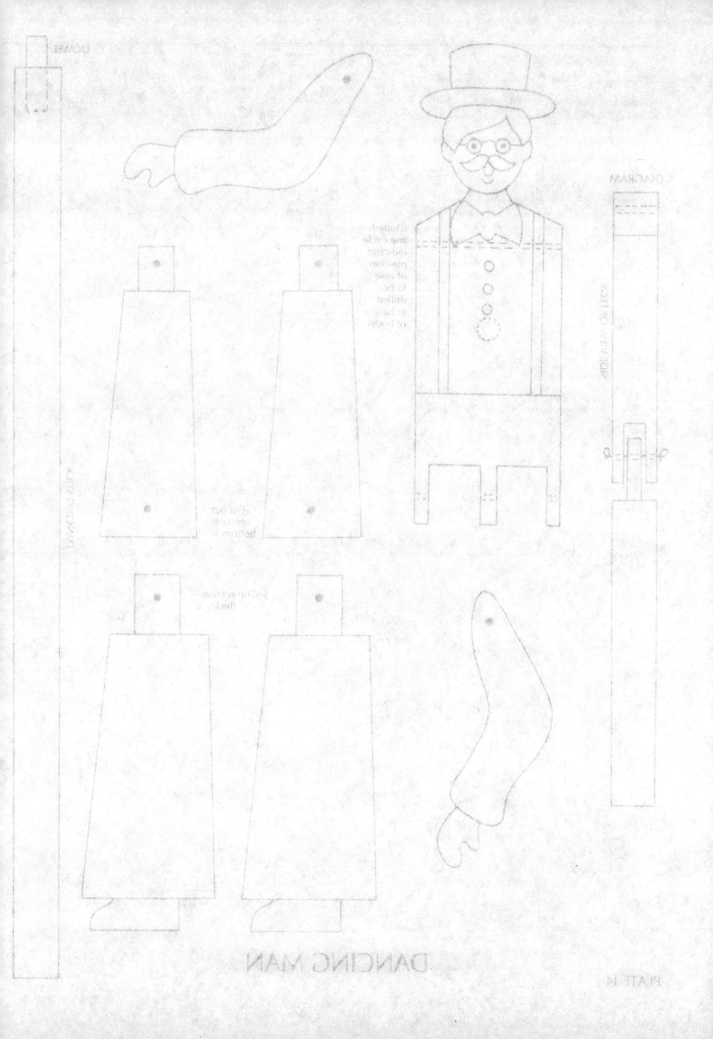

DANCING MAN

DOWEL

DIAGRAM

DANCING MAN

PLATE 14

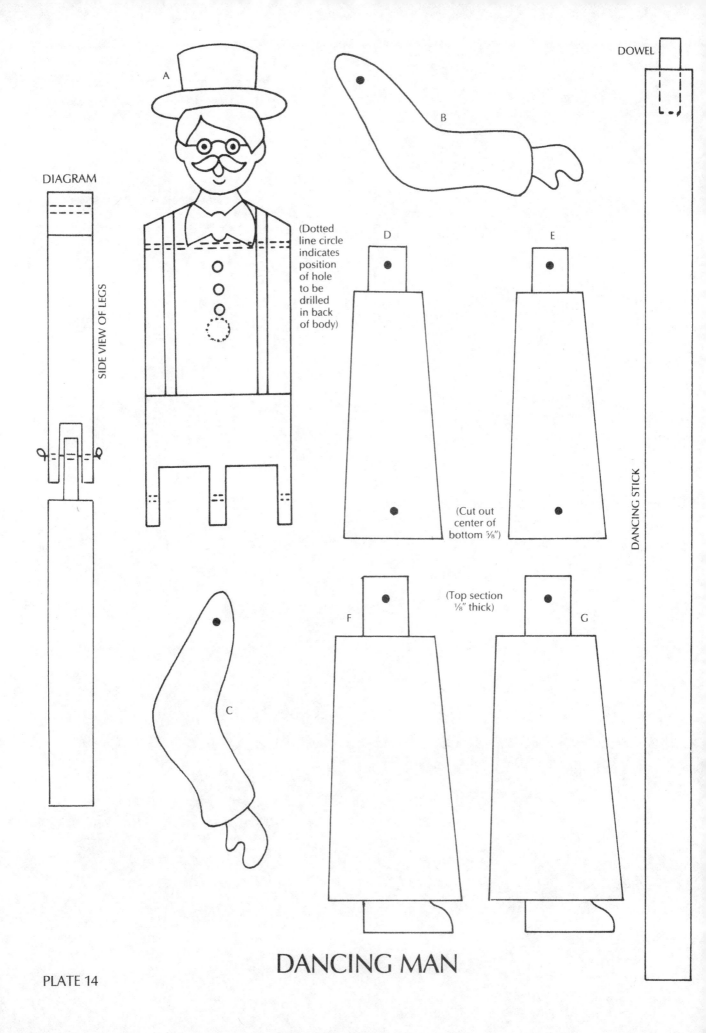

DIAGRAM

SIDE VIEW OF LEGS

A

B

(Dotted line circle indicates position of hole to be drilled in back of body)

C

D

E

(Cut out center of bottom ⅝")

F

(Top section ⅛" thick)

G

DOWEL

DANCING STICK

DANCING MAN

PLATE 14

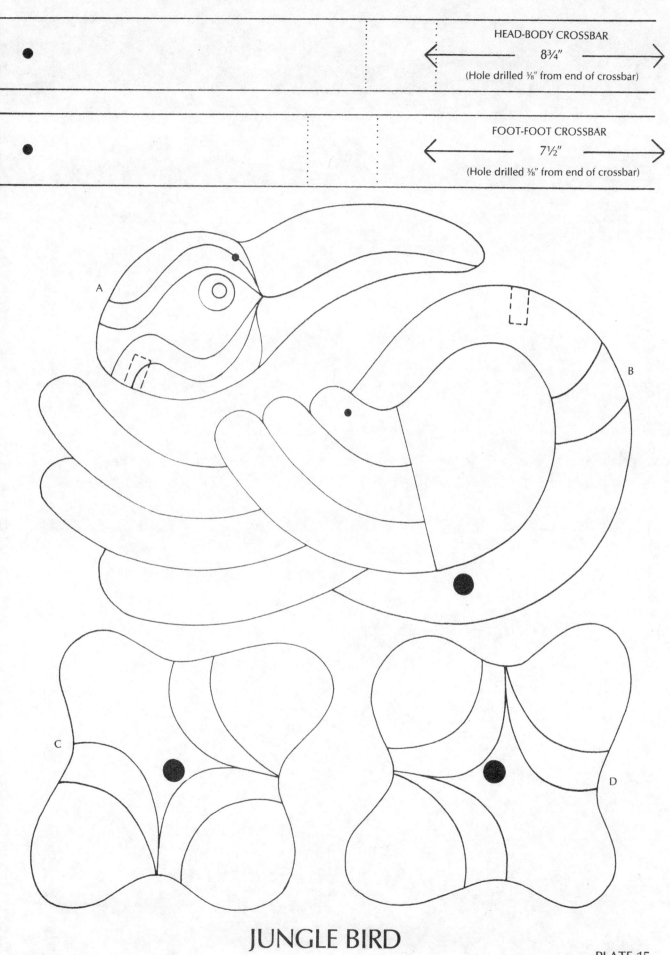

HEAD-BODY CROSSBAR

8¾"

(Hole drilled ⅜" from end of crossbar)

FOOT-FOOT CROSSBAR

7½"

(Hole drilled ⅜" from end of crossbar)

A

B

C

D

JUNGLE BIRD

PLATE 15

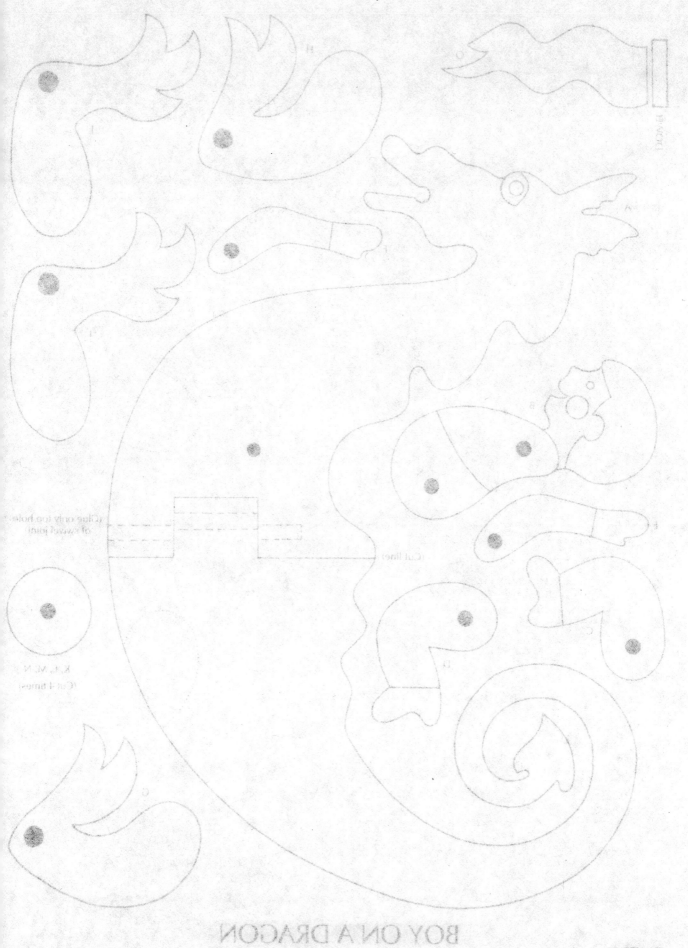

BOY ON A DRAGON

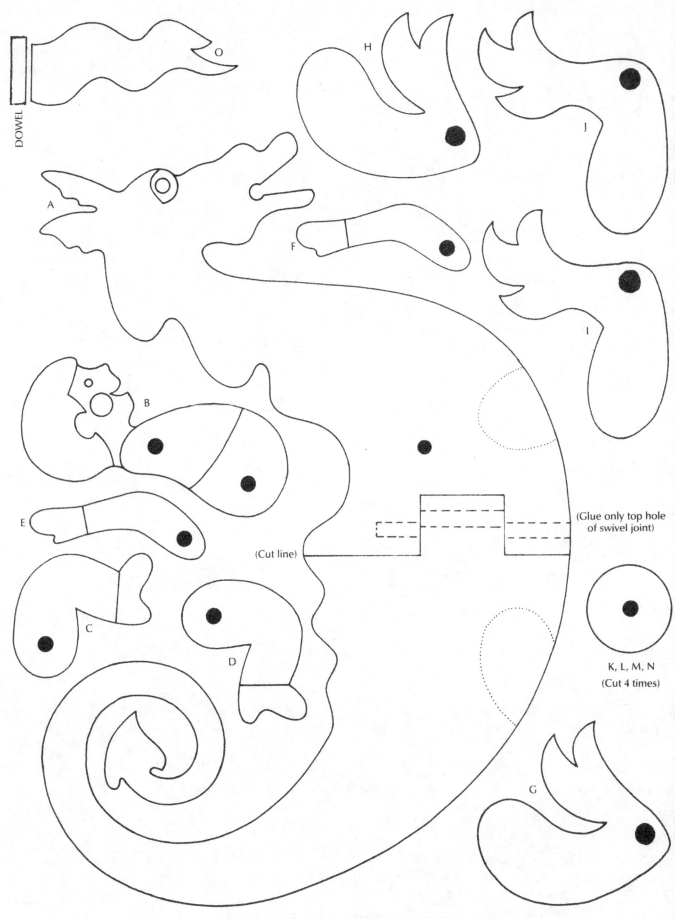

DOWEL

O

H

J

A

I

F

B

E

C

D

(Cut line)

(Glue only top hole
of swivel joint)

K, L, M, N

(Cut 4 times)

G

BOY ON A DRAGON

PLATE 16

ACROBAT CLOWN

(The transfer patterns for this toy are printed on Plate 9.)

Here is the acrobat clown. Squeeze the lower handles of the framework and he performs all sorts of difficult acrobatic feats of strength and agility. Squeezing the handles twists the strings, and the clown appears to tumble and swing.

5 pattern pieces, 2 sticks, a crossbar, 2 pieces of heavy wire, a piece of string, 2 small thin-gauge nails (¾").

PATTERN KEY

Parts A–E on ⅛" wood, trapeze squeeze sticks and crossbar are cut from ½" wood.

A. clown's body	B, C. clown's arms	D, E. clown's legs

Two trapeze squeeze sticks 13" × ½" × ⁵⁄₁₆"; one crossbar 2½" × ½" × ½".

Dots indicate ³⁄₃₂" holes to be drilled in clown pieces and through ⁵⁄₁₆" depth on squeeze sticks.
Dotted line indicates position to nail crossbar between squeeze sticks.

1. Transfer all patterns onto wood of specified thickness.
2. Cut out all wood pattern pieces and cut sticks and crossbars of specified size.
3. Trace paint lines onto opposite sides of clown pieces.
4. Drill holes where indicated by dots.
5. Sand rough edges on wood pieces.
6. Paint all wood pattern pieces.
7. Attach arms and legs to clown body. Cut 1" piece of wire and bend one end over to form a knot. Insert other end of wire through holes in arm and body pieces and bend it into a knot. Cut second piece of wire and repeat procedure for legs.
8. Attach crossbar between squeeze sticks where marked (8" from holes-end of stick) with a nail in each side. Do not nail pieces together too tightly or you will not be able to squeeze the sticks properly.
9. Follow diagram when stringing clown to trapeze frame. Lay clown on face and place hands between squeeze sticks. Insert string through the two holes in each of the sticks and hands as shown. Tie a knot in string ends when done, leaving ¾" of string projecting to secure knot.

(Continued from page 8)

BABY BUGGY

(The transfer patterns for this toy are printed on Plate 10.)

8 pattern pieces, 3 dowels.

PATTERN KEY

A. baby buggy middle section, ¾"

B, C. baby buggy outside sections, ³⁄₃₂"

D, E. handles, ¼"

F, G. front wheels, ½"

H, I. back wheels, ½"

Two ³⁄₁₆" dowels of 1¾" length for wheels; one ³⁄₁₆" dowel of 1½" length for handles.

Dots indicate ³⁄₁₆" holes to be drilled in wheels and handles and ¼" holes in buggy sections.

Dotted lines indicate position for gluing handles on buggy's outside sections.

1. Transfer all patterns onto wood of specified thickness.

2. Cut out all wood pattern pieces. The baby will need to be cut out of buggy's middle section.

3. Trace paint lines onto opposite side of baby and dotted glue lines onto the opposite side of one outside buggy section.

4. Cut dowels.

5. Drill holes where indicated by dots.

6. Sand rough edges on wood pieces.

7. Glue the outside buggy sections to each side of the middle section, making sure that dotted glue lines are showing on both outside surfaces.

8. Sand buggy edges again.

9. Paint all wood pattern pieces.

10. Glue handles to buggy where indicated by dotted lines.

11. Assemble buggy by placing dowels in appropriate holes. The baby should be placed in hole in buggy.

HARLEQUIN ACROBAT

(The transfer patterns for this toy are printed on Plate 11.)

The harlequin climbs and somersaults when the long dowel stick is moved up and down.

5 pattern pieces, 2 dowel sticks, a wood block, 4 pieces of heavy wire.

PATTERN KEY

Parts A–E on ¼" wood, wood block is cut from ¾" wood.

A. body   B. left leg   C. right leg
D. right arm   E. left arm

Two ¼" dowels, of 9" and 18" lengths; one wood block 1½" × 1½" × ¾".

Dashed lines indicate holes to be drilled in side surface of wood block, ¼" hole for 9" dowel and ⁹⁄₃₂" or ⁵⁄₁₆" hole for 18" dowel.
Dots indicate ³⁄₃₂" holes to be drilled in harlequin pieces and dowels.

1. Transfer all patterns onto wood of specified thickness.
2. Cut out all wood pattern pieces.
3. Trace paint lines onto opposite sides of pieces.
4. Drill holes where indicated by dashed lines and dots.
5. Sand rough edges on wood pieces.
6. Paint all wood pattern pieces.
7. Glue 9" dowel into its hole in wood block with hole in dowel facing the longer of the block's top edges.
8. Attach arms and legs to harlequin body. Cut 1½" piece of heavy wire and bend one end over to form a knot. Insert other end through holes in arms and body and bend it into a knot. Cut second piece of wire and repeat steps for legs. Cut two more pieces of wire and repeat steps for holes in hands and 9" dowel and for holes in feet and 18" dowel.

SWINGING PARROT

(The transfer patterns for this toy are printed on Plate 12.)

4 pattern pieces, 1 dowel, string.

PATTERN KEY

A. left post, ½"   B. right post, ½"   C. base, ¾"
D. parrot, ¼"

One ¼" dowel of 5" length for parrot swing bar.

Dashed lines indicate ³⁄₃₂" hole to be drilled in side surface of lower area of right post and ⁵⁄₁₆" holes in side surface of upper area of left and right posts.
Dots indicate ¼" hole to be drilled below parrot's feet and ³⁄₃₂" hole in dowel.
Dotted lines indicate position to glue posts onto platform and parrot on dowel.

1. Transfer all patterns onto wood of specified thickness.
2. Cut out all wood pattern pieces.
3. Trace paint lines onto opposite sides of posts and parrot.
4. Cut dowels.
5. Drill holes where indicated by dashed lines and dots. To give more concealment to pull string, you may wish to drill a hole between points x and y in the lower area of right post instead of where indicated by the dashed lines above point x.
6. Sand rough edges on wood pieces.
7. Paint all wood pattern pieces.
8. Glue posts to base.
9. Insert right end of dowel through left post and slide it midway to right post. Slide parrot onto dowel and glue in indicated position. Slide dowel through right post. Do *not* glue dowel to posts.
10. Tie knot in end of 18" piece of string. Thread other end of string through holes in dowel and lower area of right post.
11. Wind parrot until string has wrapped around dowel a few times.
12. Pull string and watch parrot swing.

PINOCCHIO JUMPING JACK

(The transfer patterns for this toy are printed on Plate 13.)

Jumping Jacks are one of the oldest of toys. Pinocchio jumps and dances when you pull on his string.

6 pattern pieces, 1 dowel, 4 pieces of heavy wire, string.

PATTERN KEY

All parts on ⅛" wood.

A. body
D. right leg

B. right arm
E. left leg

C. left arm
F. pull string knob

One ³⁄₁₆" dowel of 2½" length.

Dashed lines indicate ¹⁄₁₆" hole to be drilled in side surface of pull string knob.
Large dot indicates ¼" hole to be drilled for nose dowel; medium dots indicate ⅛" holes in body, arms and legs; small dots indicate ¹⁄₃₂" holes in arms and legs.

1. Transfer all pattern pieces onto wood of specified thickness.
2. Cut out all wood pattern pieces.
3. Cut dowels.
4. Drill holes where indicated by dashed lines and dots.
5. Sand rough edges on wood pieces.
6. Paint all wood pattern pieces.
7. Attach arms and legs to body. Cut ¾" piece of wire and bend one end over to form a knot. Insert other end through leg and body holes, but do not bend end into a knot yet. Repeat procedure for other leg and arms.
8. Attach string to small holes as shown in diagram. Lay Pinocchio on face with arms and legs hanging down.
(A) Tie a knot in end of 3" piece of string. Insert unknotted end through small hole in shoulder, from front to back, and then through small hole in other shoulder, from back to front. Pull string taut and tie a knot in end, trimming off excess string. Bend ends of wire in arms into knots. Repeat procedures for legs.
(B) Tie end of 8" piece of string to the middle of the arm string and then to the middle of the leg string, leaving no slack between the two knots. Insert string through hole in pull string knob and tie knot in end.
(C) Tie a 3" loop to hole in top of head.
9. Place growing dowel nose in nose hole.

DANCING MAN

(The transfer patterns for this toy are printed on Plate 14.)

This toy's arms and legs are loosely fastened by wire and he is suspended by a hand stick in his back. Touching the feet of the dancing man to a floor or table sets him into a rhythmic and realistic tap dance, tapping his feet and swinging his arms.

7 pattern pieces, 1 stick, 1 dowel, 6 pieces of heavy wire.

PATTERN KEY

A. body, ½"   B, C. arms, ¼"   D, E. upper legs, ½"
F, G. lower legs, ½"

One stick measuring 9½" × ½" × ½"; one ¼" dowel of ¾" length.

Dashed lines indicate ⅟₁₆" holes to be drilled in side surface of body and ¼" hole to be drilled in end of dancing stick.
Dots indicate ⅟₁₆" holes to be drilled in legs and arms.
Dotted line indicates position of ¼" hole to be drilled in dancing man's back.

1. Transfer all pattern pieces onto wood of specified thickness.
2. Cut out all wood pattern pieces including dancing stick. Please note ¼" × ⅝" slot to be cut in the lower part of upper leg, and the ⅛" thick section to be left at top of lower leg (remove ³⁄₁₆" on each side of section).
3. Sketch an appropriate pattern on the back of the dancing man's body.
4. Drill holes where indicated by dots and dashed lines. Drill hole in dancing man's back opposite the dotted line circle on the front.
5. Cut dowel.
6. Sand rough edges on wood pieces.
7. Paint all wood pattern pieces.
8. Assemble dancing man. Cut 1½" piece of wire and bend one end over to form a knot. Insert other end through holes for knee joint in upper and lower legs as shown in diagram. Bend wire end into knot. Follow same procedure in attaching legs to body with a 2½" piece of wire and arms to body with a 2¾" wire.
9. Glue dowel into dancing stick.
10. Glue stick into hole in dancing man's back.

JUNGLE BIRD

(The transfer patterns for this toy are printed on Plate 15.)

4 pattern pieces, 2 crossbars, 2 pieces of rope, 4 pieces of string.

PATTERN KEY

All parts on ¾" wood.

A. head   B. body   C, D. feet

Head-body crossbar measures ¼" × ¾" × 8¾"; foot-foot crossbar measures ¼" × ¾" × 7½".

Dashed lines indicate ¼" holes to be drilled in side surface of head and body.
Dots indicate ¼" holes to be drilled in feet and body and ³⁄₃₂" holes in body, head and crossbars.
Dotted lines indicate position for gluing crossbars together.

1. Transfer all patterns onto wood of specified thickness.
2. Cut out all wood pattern pieces. The crossbars should be cut to the dimensions specified above.
3. Trace paint lines onto opposite sides of pieces.
4. Drill holes where indicated by dots. The crossbars should be drilled ⅜" from each end.
5. Sand rough edges on wood pieces.
6. Paint all wood pattern pieces.
7. Glue crossbars together where indicated by dotted line.
8. Glue ends of 5" piece of rope into holes in side surfaces of head and body. Insert 12½" piece of rope into large hole under the wings. The ends of the rope can be inserted in foot holes, *but do not glue yet.*
9. String bird to crossbars.
(A) Tie a large knot on the end of a 19" piece of string. Insert other end through a hole in the longer crossbar and bird's head and knot securely. Repeat procedure with an 18" piece of string for other hole in longer crossbar and small hole in body.
(B) Tie a large knot in a 21" piece of string and insert other end through a hole in the shorter crossbar. Glue ends of string and rope for feet into the appropriate foot hole. Repeat procedure for remaining hole in crossbar and other foot.

BOY ON A DRAGON

(The transfer patterns for this toy are printed on Plate 16.)

15 pattern pieces, 7 dowels.

PATTERN KEY

A. dragon's body, ¾″   B. boy's body, ¾″   C, D. boy's legs, ¼″
E, F. boy's arms, ¼″   G, H. dragon's back   I, J. dragon's front
                              legs, ¼″   legs, ¼″
K, L, M, N. wheels, ¼″   O. dragon's tongue, ⅛″

One ³⁄₁₆″ dowel of 2″ length for swivel joint in dragon's body; two ³⁄₁₆″ dowels of
1¾″ length for the wheels; three ³⁄₁₆″ dowels of 1¼″ length for boy's arms and legs,
and footrest for boy's feet (in dragon's body); one ⅛″ dowel of ¾″ length for tongue
dowel in dragon's mouth.

Dashed lines indicate ³⁄₁₆″ holes to be drilled for swivel joint in dragon's body.
Dots indicate ³⁄₁₆″ holes to be drilled in various parts of boy, dragon's body and
wheels and ¼″ holes in dragon's legs.
Dot lines indicate position to glue dragon's legs to body.

1. Transfer all patterns onto wood of specified thickness.
2. Cut out all wood pattern pieces. The dragon's body should be cut in two as
shown.
3. Trace paint and glue lines onto opposite sides of pieces where necessary.
4. Cut dowels.
5. Drill holes where indicated by dashed lines and dots. Note arrangement of the
three swivel joint sections in dragon's body.
6. Sand rough edges on wood pieces.
7. Paint all wood pattern pieces.
8. Glue dragon's legs to body where indicated by dotted lines. Dowel holes should
align.
9. Construct swivel joint in dragon's body. The dowel should be glued into only
the upper hole section. After hole has been glued, align the holes and insert dowel
from underneath.
10. Insert rest of dowels in appropriate holes.
11. Glue dragon's tongue to dowel and insert in dragon's mouth.
12. Attach screw eye to dragon if you wish to pull toy by string.